W9-ARG-909

COUGARS

by Arnold Ringstad

amicus
high interest

Amicus High Interest is published by Amicus
P.O. Box 1329, Mankato, MN 56002
www.amicuspublishing.us

Library of Congress Cataloging-in-Publication Data
Ringstad, Arnold, author.
  Cougars / by Arnold Ringstad.
    pages cm. -- (Wild cats)
  Summary: "Presents information about cougars, their habitats, and their special features, including their powerful jumping ability"-- Provided by publisher.
  Audience: 6.
  Audience: K to grade 3.
  Includes index.
  ISBN 978-1-60753-600-0 (hardcover) -- ISBN 978-1-60753-640-6 (pdf ebook)
  1. Puma--Juvenile literature. I. Title.
  QL737.C23R566 2014
  599.75'24--dc23
                                    2013044190

Photo Credits: MaZiKab/Shutterstock Images, cover, 16–17; Scott E. Read/Shutterstock Images, 2, 8–9; Debbie Steinhausser/Shutterstock Images, 4–5; Fuse/Thinkstock, 6–7, 23; Jeannette Katzir Photog/Shutterstock Images, 10–11, 22; ExactoStock/SuperStock, 12–13; iStockphoto/Thinkstock, 14–15; Dirk Brink/Shutterstock Images, 18–19; Beata Aldridge/Shutterstock Images, 20–21

Produced for Amicus by The Peterson Publishing Company
and Red Line Editorial.

Designer Becky Daum
Printed in the United States of America
Mankato, MN
January, 2014
PA10001
10 9 8 7 6 5 4 3 2 1

TABLE OF CONTENTS

Powerful Cats

Cougars are large cats.
They have strong muscles.
Cougars weigh ten times what
housecats do. They are also
called **mountain lions**. They
got this name for their size.

Where Cougars Live

Cougars live in North and South America. They live alone in forests. They rest in caves when it rains. The cats live in large **territories**. They hunt here. These areas are up to 135 square miles (350 sq km).

Winter and Summer

Some cougars have two territories. One is for summer. The other is for winter. They **migrate** between the territories. That way they do not get too hot or too cold.

Like a Housecat?
Housecats can jump about 8 feet (2.4 m).

Huge Leaps

Cougars can jump 18 feet (5.5 m). They use their strong legs. Cougars have wide paws. These help them leap off the ground.

Hunting

Cougars hunt deer. They sneak up on their **prey**. Then they **pounce**. Cougars bite with powerful jaws.

Fun Fact

Cougars eat about 48 deer per year.

Newborn Cougars

Baby cougars are called cubs.

Their eyes open after 10 days.

Their mother keeps them safe.

She has two or three cubs.

Fun Fact

**Young cougars have spots.
Adults do not.**

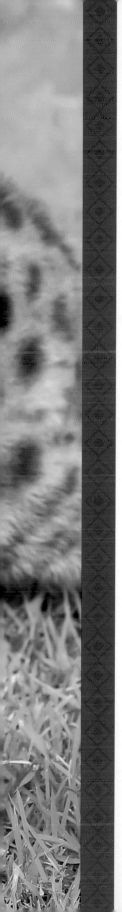

Growing Cubs

The cubs drink milk. It comes from their mother. After two months, they eat meat. Their mother teaches them to hunt. After two years, the cubs live alone.

Noisy Cougars

Cougars make noises. They sometimes whistle. Mothers growl. They warn **predators** to stay away from their cubs.

Like a Housecat?

Cougars sound like giant housecats when they growl.

Hunted Cougars

Cougars once lived across the United States. People hunted them. Today cougars do not live in the east. Some still live in the west.

Cougar Facts

Size: 64–264 pounds (29–120 kg), 34–61 inches (86–154 cm)

Range: Western North America, South America

Habitat: forests, grasslands, swamps

Number of babies: 1–6

Food: deer, moose, squirrels

Special feature: powerful legs for jumping

Words to Know

migrate – travel to live in a new place

mountain lion – a nickname for cougars

pounce – jump

predators – animals that hunt and eat
other animals

prey – animals hunted by other animals

territories – the area an animal lives in
and defends

Learn More

Books

Randall, Henry. *Cougars (Cats of the Wild)*. New York: PowerKids Press, 2011.

Rodriguez, Cindy. *Cougars (Eye to Eye with Endangered Species)*. Vero Beach, FL: Rourke Publishing, 2011.

Websites

National Geographic—Mountain Lions

http://animals.nationalgeographic.com/animals/mammals/mountain-lion

Learn more about cougars and hear the sounds they make.

San Diego Zoo—Mountain Lion (Puma, Cougar)

http://animals.sandiegozoo.org/animals/mountain-lion-puma-cougar

Read more fun facts about cougars.

Index